D0046119

Extreme Sports Stars

Philip Abraham

Children's Press®
A Division of Scholastic Inc.
New York / Toronto / London / Auckland / Sydney
Mexico City / New Delhi / Hong Kong
Danbury, Connecticut

Book Design: Dean Galiano
Contributing Editor: Geeta Sobha

Photo Credits: Photo credits: Cover © Michael Bradley/Getty Images; pgs. 4, 13 © Streeter Lecka/Getty Images; pg. 7 © Brian Bahr/Getty Images; pgs. 8, 31 © Christian Petersen/Getty Images; pg. 11 © Nick Laham/Getty Images; pg. 16 © Donald Miralle/Allsport/Getty Images; pg. 19 © Ezra Shaw/Allsport/Getty Images; pg. 21 © Amanda Edwards/Getty Images; pg. 23 © Mark Mainz /Getty Images; pg. 24 Fox Photos/Getty Images; pg. 27 AP Photo/Brian Myrick; pg. 29 © Pierre Tostee/AFP/Getty Images; pg. 32 © Susana Gonzalez/AFP/Getty Images; pg. 34 Graham Chadwick/Allsport/Getty Images; pg. 37 © Joe Klamar/AFP/Getty Images; pg. 39 © Shaun Botterill/Getty Images; pg. 40 © Tony Donaldson/Icon SMI

Library of Congress Cataloging-in-Publication Data

Abraham, Philip, 1970-
    Extreme sports stars / Philip Abraham.
    p. cm. — (Greatest sports heroes)
    Includes index.
        ISBN-10: 0-531-12585-8 (lib. bdg.)   0-531-18702-0 (pbk.)
        ISBN-13: 978-0-531-12585-4 (lib. bdg.)   978-0-531-18702-9 (pbk.)
        1. Extreme sports–Juvenile literature.   I. Title. II. Series.

    GV749.7.A37 2007
    796.04'60922-dc22

                                                    2006007155

1 2 3 4 5 6 7 8 9 10 R 11 10 09 08 07

Contents

Introduction

You are at the starting line. Your motocross bike edges forward, as though it has a mind of its own. The starting flag drops. All the bikes roar to life in unison, then shoot past the starting line like missiles. You are ahead of the pack, taking the curves of the track without slowing down. It's a dangerous move, but worth the risk. In this race, every second counts. You shoot over dirt hills, flying into the air like Superman. The crowd is on its feet. They are amazed.

To your left, the riders in the second and third positions are closing in on you. Either one could overtake you and win the race. Suddenly, as the third racer tries to pass the second, he loses control of his bike. It flips over, sending him crashing into the second rider. You don't look back—to do so would risk losing your concentration and maybe even

Motocross competitor Travis Pastrana performs at the Moto X Freestyle during the X Games.

the race. However, today is your day of victory. You are first across the finish line. You have just won your first motocross event!

Motocross, along with BMX riding, skateboarding, and snowboarding, is an action sport that pushes athletes to their mental and physical extremes. Extreme sports athletes develop many technical skills and have nerves of steel. So who are the top athletes of skateboarding, BMX riding, motocross, and snowboarding? Get ready to meet the athletes who take sports to the extreme limits!

Shaun White performs a trick at the Chevrolet U.S. Snowboard Grand Prix in 2005.

Skateboarding started in the 1950s when surfers took their sport to the streets. Competitive skateboarding began in 1963. Over the years, skateboarders have developed new styles and tricks. Alan Gelfand invented the ollie in 1978, and later Mark Gonzales ollied up a curb and jumped a set of stairs.

Today, skateboarders continue to thrill their fans with different styles of skateboarding. Street-style skateboarders perform stunts on objects such as curbs and benches. Vert-style tricks are done in the air. Skateboarders use large ramps called half-pipes to build up speed by rolling from one side of the ramp to the other. Then they leap above the edge of the ramp, high into the air, and perform tricks. Bob Burnquist, Andy MacDonald, and Elissa Steamer are three athletes who have taken skateboarding to new heights.

The ability to land amazing jumps, as shown here, won Elissa Steamer the gold medal at the X Games in 2005.

Bob Burnquist

Bob Burnquist was born and raised in Sao Paulo, Brazil. He was born on October 10, 1976. Burnquist started skateboarding at the age of eleven. He took part in hundreds of vert competitions before turning professional at the age of fourteen.

Burnquist skates both regular and goofy-footed styles. That means he can do his tricks

The Meaning of Extreme

goofy-footed when a skateboarder or snowboarder rides with his or her right foot forward on the board

kickflip the skateboard is kicked into a spin while the skater is in the air

ollies when the back of the skateboard is snapped down and the skateboarder jumps up as the front goes up

shifties the upper and lower body are twisted in different directions and the front leg is straight out

vert short for vertical; tricks that are done using ramps or pipes that allow the rider to do stunts straight up in the air

In 2006, Bob came in second place at the Mega Ramp Competition in Mexico City.

backward and forward. One of his most exciting tricks is a full loop in a 12-foot (3 meters) pipe. Burnquist has won dozens of awards. In March 2006, he skated a 40-foot (12 m) ramp, which led to a 40-foot rail jump that ended with a parachute jump into the Grand Canyon.

What makes his athletic accomplishments even more amazing is that Burnquist suffers from asthma. Still, he does not allow his illness to stop him from achieving his goals.

Burnquist's talents are not limited to skating. He has designed skate ramps, started his own organic food company, and is a licensed pilot.

Andy MacDonald

Andy MacDonald was born on July 31, 1973, in Boston, Massachusetts. He started skateboarding in 1986. He and his brother practiced together. Andy's father took the brothers on a tour of the major skate parks in the United States. Though he participated in high school sports, Andy was more attracted to skateboarding. He liked not having a set training schedule or a coach telling him how to train.

In 1994, Andy became a professional skateboarder. He is well-known for riding

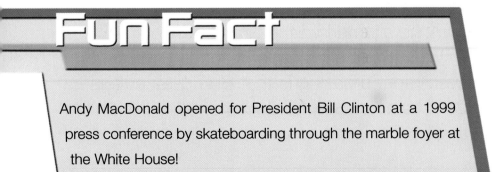

Fun Fact

Andy MacDonald opened for President Bill Clinton at a 1999 press conference by skateboarding through the marble foyer at the White House!

Andy spends about six hours a day on his board. No wonder he now has sixteen X Games medals.

ramps and the half-pipe. He also likes to skate stairs and handrails as well as the walls of empty swimming pools. In 1997, Andy became the first person to do a back flip on a skateboard.

Andy does not have a set training routine. However, he does skate a lot—sometimes as much as 8 hours a day! It has paid off: Andy's greatest achievements include winning the World Cup overall combined title for eight straight years. He is also the only skater in the World Cup to compete in both street- and vert-styles categories.

Elissa Steamer

Elissa Steamer is one of the first professional female skateboarders. Steamer was born on July 31, 1975, in Fort Myers, Florida. She

Fun and Games

Skateboarding, BMX riding, motocross, and snowboarding have made their way into pop culture. There are several video games that feature these extreme sports and their athletes. Among the video games are: *Tony Hawk Pro Skater, Dave Mirra Freestyle BMX,* and *Mat Hoffman's Pro BMX.*

Hollywood has also taken notice of extreme athletes. They star in movies such as *Ultimate X* (an IMAX film) and *The White Album* (2004), a showcase for snowboarder Shaun White. BMX rider Mat Hoffman has worked in Hollywood on the movie *XXX*, a spy film starring Vin Diesel.

started skateboarding when she was about fourteen years old.

Steamer turned professional in April 1998 and won the first women's street competition at the Slam City Jam in Vancouver, British Columbia, Canada. After several competitions, Steamer was sponsored by a skateboard company. They featured Steamer in a skate video. Soon, other sponsors were approaching her to use their gear.

She was the first female skateboarder ever to take X-Game Gold. She took gold medals at the Summmer X Games in 2004 and in 2005 by landing tricks and stunts like ollies, shifties, kickflips and more. She can do it all.

Chapter Two

BMX Riding

BMX is short for bicycle motocross. Motocross is a motorcycle race that takes place on a rough course with features such as steep drops and sharp turns. BMX athletes use bicycles instead of motorcycles. BMX started in California in the 1960s. Kids used their bikes to imitate stunts performed by their favorite motocross riders. As bicycle motocross developed, BMX riders pushed themselves and their competition to invent gravity-defying stunts.

BMX riders use specially designed bikes with 20-inch (51 centimeters) wheels. These are smaller than the 26-inch (66 cm) wheels on most mountain bikes. These sturdy bikes are used to perform stunts on dirt tracks. Dave Mirra, Mat Hoffman, and Ryan Nyquist are three of today's top BMX riders.

The athletes featured in this section are all BMX stunt riders. There are different types of

BMX races are between 25 to 40 seconds long. Riders can move as fast as 35 miles (56 kilometers) per hour.

stunt competitions: street, vert, and dirt. In street, riders show off creative stunts on banks, rails, walls, or anything else they come across.

Vert riders jump from one side of a half-pipe to the other side, and perform tricks in the air. They can also perform tricks on the lip of the half-pipe. After their performance, the rider moves down into the U of the half-pipe.

Dirt riders do tricks on dirt areas that consist of mounds separated by deep gaps.

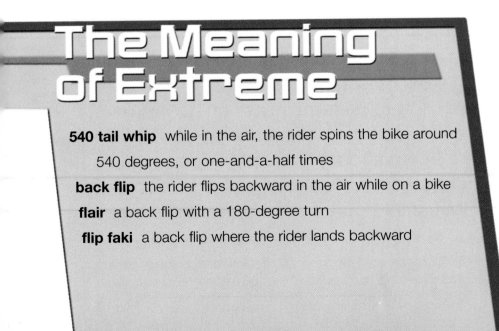

The Meaning of Extreme

540 tail whip while in the air, the rider spins the bike around 540 degrees, or one-and-a-half times

back flip the rider flips backward in the air while on a bike

flair a back flip with a 180-degree turn

flip faki a back flip where the rider lands backward

Dave was the first BMX rider to land a double back flip in competition.

Dave Mirra

Dave Mirra was born on April 4, 1974. He grew up in Chittenango, New York. He is one of the most successful BMX riders ever. When he was about eight years old, Mirra and his older brother, Tim, discovered BMX. They taught themselves freestyle tricks. They jumped curbs, mounds of dirt, and even built wooden ramps that they used to launch themselves into the air.

Mirra practiced every day on his bike. Soon his riding skills won national attention. He even made friends with BMX legend Dennis McCoy, his personal hero. Mirra appeared in his first competition, Dorkin' in York 2, at thirteen years old. His exciting riding style got him a major sponsor. By then, Mirra had expanded into vert riding. He pushes his own limits with double back flips and 540 tail whips.

Dave turned professional in 1992. At eighteen years old, Mirra broke Mat Hoffman's three-year winning streak. Then, a tragic accident in December 1993 almost ended Dave Mirra's career—and even his life.

Mirra was hit by a drunk driver. He suffered a fractured skull and torn shoulder. He had to fight for his life, and it took months of medical attention before he was well enough to ride

Fun Fact

Dave Mirra is the most decorated bike stunt rider in X Games history. He has fourteen medals, of which eleven are gold.

Mat's nickname is the Condor. He is known for doing stunts on the half-pipe.

again. In his first competition since the accident, Mirra won first place in street riding and third in vert at the 1994 Chicago Bicycle Stunt Series.

Mat Hoffman

Mat Hoffman was born on January 9, 1972, in Edmond, Oklahoma. He has ten World Champion vert titles. Hoffman began competing as an amateur on the freestyle

BMX circuit when he was thirteen years old. By the time he was sixteen, he was the youngest professional BMX rider.

Hoffman has invented more than one hundred tricks, including the flip faki, and the flair. In 2002, he set a record by successfully completing the first-ever no-handed 900 at the 2002 X Games. This feat helped him win a silver medal.

Mat owns Hoffman Sports Association. This company produces bike events, such as the X Games, around the world. He has produced, directed, and hosted TV shows for ESPN.

Ryan Nyquist

Ryan Nyquist was born on March 6, 1979, in Los Gatos, California. He entered his first freestyle BMX dirt contest when he was sixteen years old. In 1996, he turned professional. Nyquist has competed in all three types of freestyle BMX competition: dirt, park, and vert. He has won medals at the X Games and the Gravity Games.

Ryan soars high above the crowd at a competition in New York City in 2003.

Nyquist's success on his bike has led to success in the business world. He has his own signature shoe as well as trading cards, action figures, and bikes. Nyquist has been featured on TV shows such as Nickelodeon's *Game and Sports Show*. He has worked with charities such as the Make-A-Wish Foundation and the GPX Skatepark Charity Jam.

Chapter Three

Motocross

Motocross is motorcycle racing over rough land that has hills, muddy areas, and difficult turns. The name motocross combines the words "motorcycle" and "cross country." Motocross bikes are classified by their engine sizes, such as 125cc and 250cc. The cc stands for cubic centimeters. The sport started in Europe after World War II. In the United States, it got popular in the 1960s.

There are different kinds of motocross events. Freestyle motocross does not focus on racing. It is all about doing acrobatic stunts while jumping the motocross bikes into the air. Supermotocross is where a motocross race takes place on a track that is part concrete and part off-road, or rough surface. James Stewart, Jr., Ricky Carmichael, and Travis Pastrana are three of motocross's most popular athletes.

Motocross was started in England. It was called scrambles.

James Stewart, Jr.

James Stewart, Jr., was born on December 21, 1985, in Bartow, Florida. In 1993, Stewart signed with his first sponsor, Kawasaki—at just seven years old! Young riders do not need a license to practice motocross. Stewart started out in the 125cc division and went on to earn the best record ever in the division. In 2001, he captured his eleventh AMA (American Motorcyclist Association) Amateur National Championship. This victory allowed

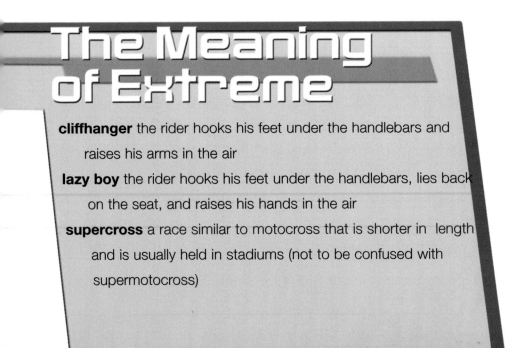

The Meaning of Extreme

cliffhanger the rider hooks his feet under the handlebars and raises his arms in the air

lazy boy the rider hooks his feet under the handlebars, lies back on the seat, and raises his hands in the air

supercross a race similar to motocross that is shorter in length and is usually held in stadiums (not to be confused with supermotocross)

James practices every day from about 9:30 A.M. until about 4:00 P.M.

him to pass Ricky Carmichael as the amateur rider with the most wins ever.

Stewart is the first African American to win a major motosports championship. In 2002, he became the youngest rider ever to win a supercross race. Months later, he became the youngest rider ever to win a motocross championship—the AMA Motocross Nationals—when he took his first AMA 125cc national title.

Stewart takes motocross very seriously. He is always working hard to become an even better athlete. He studies films of his races, looking for things to improve so he can be the best rider he can be.

Ricky Carmichael

Ricky Carmichael is the most successful motocross racer of all time. Carmichael was born on November 27, 1979, in Clearwater, Florida. He began racing when he was five years old. His parents were and are very supportive of his motocross career. His mother would drive him to competitions when he was a child. When he was nine years old, Ricky's mother sent his racing profile to a company that makes motocross clothing. They agreed to be his sponsor.

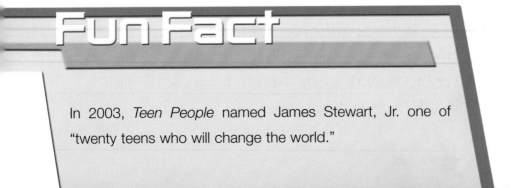

Fun Fact

In 2003, *Teen People* named James Stewart, Jr. one of "twenty teens who will change the world."

Ricky Carmichael, shown here at the Supercross U.S. Open, won twenty-two out of twenty-four outdoor events in 2005.

Carmichael started riding professionally in 1996. He won the 125 National Motocross Championship every year from 1997 to 1999. In 2001, he won the Supercross Championship. Ricky continued to race to the top of the motocross scene. The next year, 2002, he won every 250 National Championship race—this was the first perfect season in motocross history!

Travis Pastrana

Travis Pastrana was born on October 8, 1983, in Annapolis, Maryland. He is one of the best freestyle riders in motocross. He is a five-time National Amateur Champion. Under his father's guidance, Pastrana started motocross when he was only four years old.

He entered his first 125cc race when he was thirteen years old. He became a world freestyle champion at the age of fourteen. At fifteen, he won gold medals at both the X Games and the Gravity Games.

Pastrana's signature move is a one-handed fender grab. While in the air, he scissor-kicks his legs out, grabbing the handlebars with one hand and the rear fender with the other.

Fun Fact

Travis finished school three years early. He graduated high school at the age of fifteen with a 3.9 grade point average!

Pastrana wows the crowd with jumps that can be as high as 150 feet (45 m).

Pastrana sometimes uses BMX bikes to work out his motocross stunts. He has invented about ten tricks including the lazy boy and the cliffhanger. He was the first rider to land a back flip during a competition.

Travis performs at a freestyle motocross show in Mexico City, Mexico, in 2006.

Extreme Pain

Every sport has the risk of physical injuries. Skateboarding, BMX riding, motocross, and snowboarding are no exceptions. Sometimes, the injuries can be far worse than just a few cuts and bruises.

Bob Burnquist (Skateboarding)

In 2003, trying to conquer a loop, Burnquist broke his right foot and sprained his left ankle, leaving him off his board for months.

Mat Hoffman (BMX)

During his career, Hoffman has had many serious injuries and has had seventeen operations. One accident caused internal bleeding and left Hoffman in a coma.

Travis Pastrana (Motocross)

At fourteen years old, Pastrana did not gain enough speed for a 120-foot (36.5 m) jump. He crashed into the ramp. His spine was dislocated. He was in intensive care for three weeks and a wheelchair for three months. Pastrana has also had eighteen concussions and eleven knees injuries.

Tara Dakides (Snowboarding)

Dakides's snowboarding rides have resulted in a fractured back, a broken leg, and dislocated elbows. Her most famous accident happened in 2004 on *The Late Show with David Letterman*. She dropped 25 feet (7.6 m) while attempting a stunt without her helmet and ended up with a concussion and stitches in her head.

Snowboarding began in the 1960s. It is a winter sport that mixes downhill skiing with elements of surfing and skateboarding. Tom Sims, Jake Burton, and Dimitrije Milovich developed the first ideas for snowboards. After the boards underwent technical improvements in the 1980s, the sport grew in popularity. Ski resorts began to allow snowboarding on their slopes. Movies about snowboarding also helped boost the sport's appeal.

Snowboarders ride specially designed boards down snow-covered mountain courses. Freestyle snowboarders perform tricks using half-pipe ramps that are a lot like the ones skateboarders use. Shaun White, Chris Klug, and Tara Dakides are three snowboarders who have brought this sport to new heights of popularity.

Snowboarding became part of the Winter Olympic Games in 1998.

Shaun White

Shaun White was born on September 3, 1986, in Carlsbad, California. Snowboarding was a favorite family pastime when he was a kid. He started snowboarding at the age of six. White turned professional at thirteen years old when a company that manufactures snowboards became his sponsor.

White is also a professional skateboarder. In fact, he is the first athlete to compete at both the Winter and Summer X Games. White is known for getting big air and putting together snowboarding tricks in ways no other

The Meaning of Extreme

big air when a rider makes a move that allows him or her to lift high into the air

slalom a course with a series of gates set up in combination to test the speed and agility of athletes

The Flying Tomato gets big air at the half-pipe competition in Torino, Italy.

professional snowboarder has ever done. He won two gold medals in the 2003 Winter X Games. White also won a gold medal in the 2006 Winter Olympics in Torino, Italy.

Fun Fact

White's signature feature is his long red hair. That's how he got his nickname, the Flying Tomato.

Chris Klug

Chris Klug was born in Vail, Colorado, on November 18, 1972 and moved to Oregon in 1976. He started snowboarding in 1983. He eventually took part in the Northwest Race Series. There he won most of the events and was the Northwest Series Overall Champion for two years. His first major competition was the North American Championship at Sunshine Village, Banff, Canada. He came in second in the junior half-pipe competition. He became a full-time professional snowboarder in 1991.

On July 28, 2000, Klug had a liver transplant, without which he would have died. Chris feels like he has been given a second chance to live. He was up and snowboarding seven weeks after his operation! Six months later, he won a World Cup Race in Kronplatz, Italy.

Chris went on to win the bronze medal in the 2002 Winter Olympics at Salt Lake City, Utah. He is the only organ transplant recipient to ever win an Olympic medal. Though Chris did not make it to the 2006 Winter Olympics, he is still competing strongly.

1998

This photograph shows Chris taking on the men's giant slalom in the 1998 Winter Olympics.

Tara Dakides

Tara Dakides was born on August 20, 1975, in Mission Viejo, California, and grew up in Laguna Hills, CA. Dakides started skiing when she was thirteen years old. She then went on to skateboarding, surfing, and snowboarding. Tara's style is goofy-footed.

Tara has won five gold medals at the X Games. In the early days of her career, Dakides felt lucky when a sponsor offered

Here's Tara in action at the ESPN X-Games in San Diego, California.

her a free pair of goggles. Today, her many sponsors are some of the largest companies in America who provide her with the best in boarding gear.

Dakides has put her snowboarding knowledge into creating signature sport clothing, a snowboard, and snowboard boots. She is also involved with Surfrider's Foundation, an organization that works to protect the environment.

Extreme Expense—The Cost of Extreme Sports

Skateboarding, BMX riding, motocross, and snowboarding require special equipment and clothing. This gear can be expensive. Most athletes find sponsors to supply them with equipment in exchange for the athlete promoting the company's products. Here is a sampling of the costs for each sport.

Skateboarding

Skateboarding equipment is the least expensive of the extreme sports. On average, a complete skateboard goes for around $100. Skateboarding helmets and pads can add another $50 to $100 to the price.

BMX

BMX bikes come in a variety of styles and models. A professional-style bike can go for $800 and up.

Motocross

Motocross is one of the most expensive of the extreme sports. Costs for motocross bikes can start from $1,000. Some bikes can cost more than $7,000. Motocross helmets can be about $200 to more than $500. Specially made protective shirts and pants cost another $200 or $300.

Snowboarding

Snowboards cost between $200 and $600—sometimes more. Snowboarders wear special gloves, boots, and clothing. Boots and gloves can be about $200. Jackets can cost as much as $400.

New Words

amateur (**am**-uh-chur) someone who takes part in a sport for pleasure rather than for money

coma (**koh**-muh) a state of deep unconsciousness from which it is very hard to wake up

concussion (**kuhn**-kush-**uhn**) an injury to the brain caused by a heavy blow to the head

dislocated (diss-**loh**-kate-uhd) when a bone has moved out of its usual place

extreme (ek-**streem**) exciting and very dangerous

freestyle (**free**-stile) a style found in skateboarding, BMX riding, motocross, and snowboarding that involves ground and air tricks

internal (in-**tur**-nuhl) inside someone or something

New Words

professional (pruh-**fesh**-uh-nuhl) someone who makes money for doing something as a career

profile (**proh**-file) a brief account of someone's history

ramp (**ramp**) a straight or curved slope on which skateboarders, BMX riders, and snowboarders perform tricks

sponsor (**spon**-sur) a company that pays athletes to use or promote their products

transplant (**transs**-plant) a medical operation in which a diseased organ is replaced with a healthy one

vert (**vurt**) tricks that are done on ramps or pipes that allow the rider to do stunts straight up in the air.

For Further Reading

DiGeronimo, Theresa Foy, and Andy MacDonald. Dropping in with Andy Mac: *The Life of a Pro Skateboarder.* New York: Simon and Schuster, 2003.

Hoffman, Mat, with Mark Lewman. *Ride of My Life.* New York: HarperCollins, 2002.

Klug, Chris. *To the Edge and Back.* New York: Carroll & Graf Publishers, 2004.

Mirra, Dave. Mirra Images: *The Story of My Life.* New York: HarperCollins, 2003.

Nelson, Julie. *BMX Racing and Freestyle.* Austin, TX: Raintree Steck-Vaughn Publishers, 2002.

Resources

ORGANIZATIONS

AMA Pro Racing
13515 Yarmouth Drive
Pickerington, OH 43147
(614) 856-1900
http://www.amaproracing.com

National Bicycle League, Inc.
3958 Brown Park Drive, Suite D
Hillard, Ohio 43026
1-800-886-BMX1
http://www.nbl.org

Skatepark Association of USA
2118 Wilshire Blvd. #622
Santa Monica, CA 90403
(310) 398-7112
http://www.spausa.org

Resources

About: Snowboarding
http://snowboarding.about.com/

Dave Mirra's Official Freestyle BMX Web Site
http://www.davemirra.com/
Read all about Dave Mirra on this site and find out what he is up to these days.

Kidz World: Great Moments in Skateboarding History
http://www.kidzworld.com/site/p6543.htm
Log on and read this informative article about skateboarding and much more.

X Games
http://expn.go.com/expn/index
Get information on the X Games as well as your favorite extreme sports athletes.

Index

Index

ABOUT THE AUTHOR

Philip Abraham is a freelance writer. He has written many books for children and young adults.